DISCOVERING NEWFOUNDLAND AND LABRADOR

BRIAN C. BURSEY

Printed and bound in Canada by Friesens.

ISBN 978-1-55383-154-9

Cover: Tilting, Fogo Island. Albert Dwyer's twine store is representative of many traditional buildings in Tilting.

Right: The Spout. This prominent landmark, located midway between Bay Bulls and Petty Harbour, occurs when waves in a nearby sea cave force salt water and mist from a vent in the bedrock. During heavy wells, the 'Spout' can be seen for many miles out to sea.

◄ Cape Race. One of the most powerful in the world, this lighthouse was built in 1907 as a beacon for trans-Altlantic shipping.

Iceberg at St. John's. Most Newfoundland and Labrador icebergs originate from glaciers on the west coast of Greenland. This iceberg, which towers approximately 50 metres above the water, is larger than most. Seven-eighths of its bulk remain underwater.

▶ Lighthouse at Redmonds Head, Bell Island.

Bonavista

► Fishing boats, Bell Island.

Playful humpback whales are common in Newfoundland and Labrador waters during the summer months. Adults can reach 15 metres in lenghth.

◄ Arch at Skerwink Head, near Aquaforte.

Grandys Brook, southwestern Newfoundland.

Sandy Cove. This sandy beach is one of several on the Eastport Peninsula.

◄ Cape Spear. This lighthouse, located near the most easterly point in North, America, has marked the approaches to St. John's Harbour since 1835.

▶ Signal Hill, St. John's. Cabot Tower was erected in 1897 to commemorate the 400th anniversary of John Cabot's historic voyage.

Gus, near Bonavista. Newfoundland dogs, equally at home on land or in the water, are famous for their loyalty and gentle nature.

◄ An offshore supply vessel passes below Signal Hill as it enters the harbour at St. John's.

Houses cling to sheer cliffs of the Battery, near the entrance to St. John's harbour.

St. John's is well known
for its colourful houses.

► Historic buildings in downtown St. John's
leads up to *The Rooms,* Newfoundland and
Labrador's main museum and archives
complex.

► St. Luke's Anglican Church (1895), Newtown, Bonavista Bay.

Autumn morning, St. Alban's, Bay d'Espoir.

► White birch and wild maple, central Newfoundland.

Stag Caribou.

Wild flowers, Trans-Canada Highway.

◄ Fall colours, Port Blandford.

Thunder Brook, near Grand Falls.

Moose. Native to Labrador, this non-indigenous species was first introduced to the Island in 1878.

Iceberg, Conception Bay.

◄ Sea stack, Bell Island, Newfoundland.

Fishing premises at Change Islands.

◄ Fishing boats at Frenchman's Cove,
Bay of Islands.

The Arches, a provincially maintained public beach, is located just outside the northern boundary of Gros Morne National Park. The site features a series of unusual wave-carved limestone formations.

▶ Western Brook Pond, Gros Morne National Park. The cliffs surrounding this glacially carved lake are more than 600 metres high.

The Tablelands overlook Bonne Bay and
the community of Woody Point.

◄ The Tablelands, Gros Morne National Park.
This area owes its distinctive colouration to
peridotite, a rusty brown rock which is toxic
to most forms of vegetation.

Historic Signal Hill overlooks the sheltered harbour at St. John's, Newfoundland and Labrador's capital and largest city.

◄ Shipwreck at Blue Beach, St. Lawrence.

Fishing gear lines the wharf at Bartletts Harbour at the close of a busy lobster fishing season.

◄ Cupids, established in 1610, is one of Newfoundland's oldest communities.

Trinity, one of Newfoundland's most historic
communities.

► The Pitcher Plant, floral emblem of
  Newfoundland and Labrador.

Sagona, a resettled fishing community in Fortune Bay.

▸ Fishing stage at Tilting, Fogo Island.

Lighthouse at Cape Bonavista, the traditional landfall of John Cabot. This lighthouse, erected in 1843, contains 200 year old lights which had been previously installed on Scotland's Inch Cape Rock.

Henley Harbour, Labrador.

Above: Harvesting ice from a small berg, Spaniard's Bay.
Left: Iceberg at Upper Amherst Cove, near Bonavista.

► The Cape St. Mary's Bird Sanctuary is home to thousands of gannets, murres and kittiwakes, as well as to the endangered harlequin duck.

Bakeapples. Called cloudberries elsewhere, bakeapples are found throughout Newfoundland and Labrador.

Polar Bear. Polar bears are relatively common
in northern Labrador throughout the year, and
are found as far south as St. John's in spring
and early summer.

Massive waves break against the cliffs at Middle Cove, near St. John's, during a winter storm.

Inuit ruins at North Arm, Torngat Mountains,
Labrador.

Ermine, northern Labrador.

Moravian Mission Station, Hebron. This large building, constructed in 1833, contained a church, classrooms, workshops, government offices, and even living quarters. Hebron has been designated as a National Historic Site.

◄ Churchill Falls. At 75 metres, Churchill Falls is substantially higher than Niagara Falls and one of the continent's largest cataracts. Originally called Grand Falls, and later Hamilton Falls, it was known only to native people until visited by John McLean of the Hudson's Bay Company in 1839. Water to the falls was largely diverted in the late 1960s for development of a 7,000,000 hp hydro-electric complex, Canada's largest construction project to that time.

The rising sun burns away a fog bank at Red Bay, Labrador. During the 1500s, as many as 2500 Basque whalers came to the Red Bay area annually to harvest bowhead and right whales.